45 Muscle Building Recipes to Gain Muscle Mass Without Shakes or Pills:

High Protein Content in Every Meal!

By

Joseph Correa

Certified Sports Nutritionist

COPYRIGHT

This publication is designed to provide accurate and authoritative information in regard to

The subject matter covered. It is sold with the understanding that neither the author nor the publisher is engaged in rendering medical advice. If medical advice or assistance is needed, consult with a doctor. This book is considered a guide and should not be used in any way detrimental to your health. Consult with a physician before starting this nutritional plan to make sure it's right for you.

ACKNOWLEDGEMENTS

The realization and success of this book could not have been possible without my family.

45 Muscle Building Recipes to Gain Muscle Mass Without Shakes or Pills:

High Protein Content in Every Meal!

By

Joseph Correa

Certified Sports Nutritionist

CONTENTS

ABOUT THE AUTHOR

As a certified sports nutritionist and professional athlete, I firmly believe that proper nutrition will help you reach your goals faster and effectively. My knowledge and experience has helped me live healthier throughout the years and which I have shared with family and friends. The more you know about eating and drinking healthier, the sooner you will want to change your life and eating habits.

Being successful in controlling your weight is important as it will improve all aspects of your life.

Nutrition is a key part in the process of getting in better shape and that's what this book is all about.

INTRODUCTION

45 Muscle Building Recipes to Gain Muscle Mass without Shakes or Pills will help you increase the amount of protein you consume per day to help increase muscle mass. These meals and the calendar will help increase muscle in an organized manner by having a schedule and knowing what you're eating. Being too busy to eat right can sometimes become a problem and that's why this book will save you time and help nourish your body to achieve the goals you want. Make sure you know what you're eating by preparing it yourself or having someone prepare it for you.

This book will help you to:

- Gain muscle fast.
- Have more energy.
- Naturally accelerate Your Metabolism to build more muscle.
- Improve your digestive system.

Joseph Correa is a certified sports nutritionist and a professional athlete.

MUSCLE BUILDING CALENDAR

Week 1

Day 1:

Early Riser Breakfast

Snack: Blueberry Yogurt

Tuna Burger and Salad

Snack: Cherry Tomatoes with Cottage Cheese

Mexican Style Protein Bowl

Day 2:

Blueberry Lemon Pancakes

Snack: Avocado on Toast

Spicy Beefsteak Kebabs

Snack: Apple and Peanut Butter

Mediterranean Fish

Day 3:

Power Bowl

Snack: Yogurt with Tropical Fruit

Stuffed Chicken Breast with Brown Rice

Snack: Bell Pepper with Cottage Cheese

Vegan Friendly Dinner

Day 4:

Almond Milk Smoothie

Snack: Cup of Popcorn

Pancetta-wrapped Pollock with Potatoes

Snack: Yogurt with Dried Goji Berries

Garlicky Hummus

Day 5

Greek Yogurt with Flaxseeds and Apple

Snack: Rice Cake with Peanut Butter

Baked Salmon with Grilled Asparagus

Snack: Celery Sticks with Goat Cheese and Green Olives

Chicken with Avocado Salad

Day 6:

Breakfast 'Pizza'

Snack: Greek Yogurt with Strawberries

Chicken Caesar Wraps

Snack: Roasted Chickpeas

Hot Cod

Day 7:

Bell Pepper Rings with 'Frit Grits'

Snack: Nut Mix

Beef and Broccoli Noodles

Snack: Ham and Celery Sticks

Arugula Chicken Salad

Week 2

Day 1:

Whey Protein Muffins

Snack: Avocado on Toast

Shrimp and Zucchini Linguine Pasta Salad

Snack: Apple and Peanut Butter

Tofu Burger

Day 2:

Mexican Mocha Breakfast

Snack: Yogurt with Dried Goji Berries

Trout with Potato Salad

Snack: Cup of Popcorn

Chicken with Pineapple and Bell Peppers

Day 3:

Smoked Salmon and Avocado with Toast

Snack: Cherry Tomatoes with Cottage Cheese

Spiced Chicken

Snack: Blueberry Yogurt

Grilled Mushroom and Zucchini Burger

Day 4:

Fruit and Peanut Butter Smoothie

Snack: Roasted Chickpeas

Mexican Bean Chili

Snack: Greek Yogurt with Strawberries

Sweet and Sour Chicken

Day 5:

Protein-packed Scramble

Snack: Bell pepper with Cottage Cheese

Turkey Meatloaf with Whole Wheat Couscous

Snack: Yogurt with Tropical Fruit

Dijon Mustard Halibut

Day 6:

Pumpkin Pie Protein Pancakes

Snack: Ham and Celery Sticks

Mediterranean Rice

Snack: Nut Mix

Tuna Melt

Day 7:

Tuna Stuffed Bell Peppers

Snack: Celery Sticks with Goat Cheese and Green Olives

Beef Meatball Pasta with Spinach

Snack: Rice Cake with Peanut Butter

Sushi Bowl

Week 3

Day 1:

High-protein Oatmeal

Snack: Cup of Popcorn

Stuffed Eggs with Pita Bread

Snack: Apple and Peanut Butter

Tray Bake Chicken

Day 2:

Early Riser Breakfast

Snack: Avocado on Toast

Beef and Broccoli Noodles

Snack: Yogurt with Dried Goji Berries

Garlicky Hummus

Day 3:

Power Bow

Snack: Greek Yogurt with Strawberries

Chicken Caesar Wraps

Snack: Cherry Tomatoes with Goat Cheese

Mediterranean Fish

Day 4:

Blueberry Lemon Pancakes

Snack: Roasted Chickpeas

Baked Salmon with Grilled Asparagus

Snack: Blueberry Yogurt

Arugula Chicken Salad

Day 5:

Greek Yogurt with Flaxseeds and Apple

Snack: Ham and Celery Sticks

Tuna Burger and Salad

Snack: Yogurt with Tropical Fruit

Chicken with Avocado Salad

Day 6:

Bell Pepper Rings with 'Frit Grits'

Snack: Bell Peppers with Cottage Cheese

Stuffed Chicken Breast with Brown Rice

Snack: Nut Mix

Hot Cod

Day 7:

Almond Milk Smoothie

Snack: Rice Cake with Peanut Butter

Spicy Beefsteak Kebabs

Snack: Celery Sticks with Goat Cheese and Green Olives

Mexican Style Protein Bowl

Week 4

Day 1:

Breakfast 'Pizza'

Snack: Greek Yogurt with Strawberries

Pancetta-wrapped Pollock with Potatoes

Snack: Cup of Popcorn

Vegan Friendly Dinner

Day 2:

Mexican Mocha Breakfast

Snack: Cherry Tomatoes with Cottage Cheese

Mediterranean Rice

Snack: Apple and Peanut Butter

Grilled Mushroom and Zucchini Burger

Day 3:

Fruit and Peanut Butter Smoothie

Snack: Avocado on Toast

Shrimp and Zucchini Linguine Pasta Salad

Snack: Blueberry Yogurt

Sweet and Sour Chicken

Day 4:

Pumpkin Pie Protein Pancakes

Snack: Yogurt with Dried Goji Berries

Spiced Chicken

Snack: Roasted Chickpeas

Dijon Mustard Halibut

Day 5:

Smoked Salmon and Avocado with Toast

Snack: Ham and Celery Sticks

Beef Meatball Pasta with Spinach

Snack: Nut Mix

Tofu Burger

Day 6:

High-protein Oatmeal

Snack: Bell Peppers with Cottage Cheese

Mexican Bean Chili

Snack: Yogurt with Tropical Fruit

Sushi Bowl

Day 7:

Protein-packed Scramble

Snack: Rice Cake with Peanut Butter

Trout with Potato Salad

Snack: Greek Yogurt with Strawberries

Tray Bake Chicken

2 extra days for a full month:

Day 1:

Whey Protein Muffins

Snack: Celery Sticks with Goat Cheese and Green Olives

Turkey Meatloaf with Whole Wheat Couscous

Snack: Apple and Peanut Butter

Tuna Melt

Day 2:

Tuna Stuffed Bell Peppers

Snack: Blueberry Yogurt

Stuffed Eggs with Pita Bread

Snack: Nut Mix

Chicken with Pineapple and Bell Peppers

45 MUSCLE BUILDING RECIPES

BREAKFAST

1.   Early Riser Breakfast

Snap your body out of a catabolic state and into a muscle-building one with this high-protein, high-carb oven-cooked breakfast. The grapefruit and asparagus make sure you get more than half a day's worth of vitamin C.

Ingredients (1serving):

6 egg whites

½ cup cooked quinoa and brown rice mix

3 asparagus spears, sliced

½ pink grapefruit

1 small red bell pepper, sliced

1 scoop flavorless whey protein powder

1 clove garlic, crushed

olive oil spray

pepper, salt

Prep time: 10 min

Cooking time: 15-20 min

Preparation:

Heat the oven to 200C fan/ gas 6. Lightly spray a cast iron skillet with olive oil.

In a medium bowl, whisk the egg whites with a pinch of salt and pepper until frothy.

Add the cooked brown rice and quinoa to the skillet; pour in the egg whites then the asparagus pieces and the bell pepper slices.

Bake in the oven for 15-20 min or until the eggs are cooked.

Nutritional value per serving: 407kcal, 52g protein, 40g carbs (5g fiber, 8g sugar), 2g fat, 15% calcium, 12% iron, 19% magnesium, 26% vitamin A, 63% vitamin C, 48% vitamin K, 12% vitamin B1, 69% vitamin B2, 26% vitamin B9.

2.   Power Bowl

A breakfast with an appropriate name, the power bowl combines high in protein egg whites with energy fueling oatmeal. The walnuts add healthy fats and the honey tops everything with a bit of sweetness.

Ingredients (1 serving):

6 egg whites

½ cup instant oatmeal, cooked

 1/8 cup walnuts

¼ cup berries

1 teaspoon raw honey

Cinnamon

Prep time: 10 min

Cooking time: 5 min

Preparation:

Whisk the egg whites until frothy then cook them in a skillet on low heat.

Combine the oatmeal and the egg whites in a bowl; add the cinnamon and raw honey and mix.

Top with berries, banana and walnuts.

Nutritional value per serving: 344kcal, 30g protein, 33g carbs (3g fiber, 23g sugar), 11g fat (2 saturated), 10% iron, 15% magnesium, 10% vitamin B1, 11% vitamin B2, 15% vitamin B5.

3.   Tuna Stuffed Bell Peppers

This is a quick and nutritious recipe that provides a massive amount of B12. High in protein, tuna is an excellent breakfast option for muscle building and if you want to add some carbs to your meal, a piece of whole wheat toast is a great choice.

Ingredients (2 servings):

2 cans of tuna in water (185g), half drained

3 hard-boiled eggs

1 spring onion, finely chopped

5 small pickles, diced

salt, pepper

4 bell peppers, halved, with the seeds cleaned

Prep time: 5 min

Cooking time: 10 min

Preparation:

Combine the tuna, eggs, spring onion, pickles and seasoning in a food processor and mix until smooth.

Fill the halves of the bell peppers with the composition and serve.

Nutritional value per serving: 480kcal, 46g protein, 16g fat (4g saturated), 8g carbs (2g fiber, 4g sugar), 28% magnesium, 94% vitamin A, 400% vitamin C, 12% vitamin E, 67% vitamin K, 18% vitamin B1, 32% vitamin B2, 90% vitamin B3, 20% vitamin B5, 56% vitamin B6, 18% vitamin B9, 284% vitamin B12.

4.   Greek Yogurt with Flaxseeds and Apple

Branch out from the traditional egg white muscle-building breakfast and try some high-protein Greek Yogurt flavored with apple. Use whole flaxseeds to maximize your fiber intake and keep them in water overnight to get them soft and easily digestible.

Ingredients (1 serving):

1 cup Greek yogurt

1 apple, thinly sliced

2 tablespoons flaxseeds

¼ teaspoon cinnamon

1 teaspoon Stevia

A sprinkle of salt

Prep time: 5 min

Cooking time: 45 min

Preparation:

Preheat the oven to 190C fan/ gas 5. Place the apple slices in a non-stick pan, sprinkle them with cinnamon, Stevia and a dash of salt, cover them and bake for 45 min/ until tender. Remove them from the oven and allow them to cool for 30 min.

Place the Greek yogurt in a bowl then top with apples and flaxseeds and serve.

Nutritional value per serving: 422kcal, 22g protein, 39g carbs (7g fiber, 22 g sugar), 21g fat (8 g saturated), 14% calcium, 22% magnesium, 14% vitamin C, 24% vitamin B1, 13% vitamin B12.

5.   Bell Pepper Rings with 'Fit Grits'

A tasty and special looking meal, the bell pepper rings with 'Fit Grits' fuel your muscles and give you enough energy to power through your day. Full of color and nutrients, this breakfast is high in vitamin B1.

Ingredients (1 serving):

6 egg whites

2 eggs

¼ cup brown rice farina

1 cup raw spinach

½ green bell pepper

1 cup of cherry tomatoes

olive oil spray

salt, pepper

Prep time: 10 min

Cooking time: 15 min

Preparation:

Whisk the egg whites with a pinch of salt and pepper until frothy. Heat some oil in a non-stick frying pan and cook the egg whites and farina. Add the spinach, mix together and cook until the spinach has wilted.

Lightly spray a skillet with olive oil and set on medium heat. Cut the bell peppers horizontally to create 2 rings, place them in the skillet and crack the eggs inside the bell peppers. Let them cook until the eggs turn white.

Place the egg-farina mixture and cooked pepper rings on a plate and serve with cherry tomatoes.

Nutritional value per serving : 495kcal, 45g protein, 45g carbs (3g fiber, 7g sugar), 11g fat (3g saturated), 9% calcium, 14% iron, 20% magnesium, 35% vitamin A, 32% vitamin C, 91% vitamin B2, 22% vitamin B5, 12% vitamin B6, 15% vitamin B12.

6. Almond Milk Smoothie

10 minutes is all you need to fix this high in vitamin D and B1 almond milk smoothie. You can fix a big batch and keep it in the freezer making this smoothie a perfect option for a quick breakfast to go.

Ingredients (2 serving):

1 cup almond milk

1 cup frozen mixed berries

1 cup spinach

1 scoop banana flavored protein powder

1 tablespoon chia seeds

Prep time: 10 min

No cooking

Preparation:

Mix all the ingredients in a blender until smooth, pour into 2 glasses and serve.

Nutritional value per serving: 295kcal, 26g protein, 32g carbs (4g fiber, 13g sugar), 9g fat, 40% calcium, 20% iron, 12% magnesium, 50% vitamin A, 40% vitamin C, 25% vitamin D, 57% vitamin E, 213% vitamin B1, 18% vitamin B9.

7.   Pumpkin Pie Protein Pancakes

Forget about flour and try oat pancakes with a delicious addition of fresh pumpkin. Topple some calorie-free syrup and enjoy a high-protein breakfast that tastes as good as a cheat meal.

Ingredients (1 serving):

1/3 cup old-fashioned oats

¼ cup pumpkin

½ cup egg whites

1 scoop cinnamon protein powder

½ teaspoon cinnamon

olive oil spray

Prep time: 5 min

Cooking time: 5 min

Preparation:

Mix all the ingredients together in a bowl. Spray a medium-sized skillet with olive oil then place on medium heat.

Pour in the batter, and once you see tiny bubbles appear on the top of the pancake, flip. When each side is golden, remove the pancake and serve.

Nutritional value per serving: 335kcal, 39g protein, 37g carbs (6g fiber, 1 g sugar), 6g fat, 14% calcium, 15% iron, 26% magnesium, 60% vitamin A, 26% vitamin B1, 37% vitamin B2, 10% vitamin B5, 31% vitamin B6.

8.   High-protein Oatmeal

Lasso in a hearty helping of carbs that will keep you satiated for hours, while the protein powder and almonds will deliver a protein-packed start to your day. If you prefer you oatmeal with a fruity taste, use banana flavored protein powder.

Ingredients (1 serving):

2 packets of instant oatmeal (28g packet)

¼ cup ground almonds

1 scoop of vanilla flavored whey protein powder

1 tablespoon cinnamon

Prep time: 5 min

Cooking time: 5 min

Preparation:

Pour the instant oatmeal into a bowl, mix with the protein powder and cinnamon. Add hot water and mix. Top with crushed almonds and serve.

Nutritional value per serving: 436kcal, 33g protein, 45g carbs (10g fiber, 4g sugar), 15g fat (1g saturated), 17% calcium, 19% iron, 37% magnesium, 44% vitamin E, 21% vitamin B1, 21% vitamin B2.

9.   Protein-packed Scramble

Feed your muscles and push through an intense workout with this 51g protein meal. These scrambled egg whites with vegetables and turkey sausage have the added value of being packed with carbs and overall high amounts of vitamins.

Ingredients (1 serving):

8 egg whites

2 link turkey sausages, chopped

1 large onion, diced

1 cup red bell peppers, diced

2 tomatoes, diced

2 cups raw spinach, chopped

1 teaspoon olive oil

salt and pepper

Prep time: 10 min

Cooking time: 10-15 min

Preparation:

Whisk the egg whites with a pinch of salt and pepper until frothy, then set aside.

Heat the oil in a large non-stick pan, drizzle the onions and peppers and sauté until they are tender. Season with salt and pepper. Add the turkey sausage and cook until it is golden brown then lower the heat and add the egg whites and scramble.

When the eggs are almost done, add the tomato and spinach, cook for 2 min and serve.

Nutritional value per serving: 475kcal, 51g protein, 37g carbs (10g fiber, 18g sugar), 10g fat (2g saturated), 14% calcium, 23% iron, 37% magnesium, 255% vitamin A, 516% vitamin C, 25% vitamin E, 397% vitamin K, 22% vitamin B1, 112% vitamin B2, 29% vitamin B3, 19% vitamin B5, 51% vitamin B6, 65% vitamin B9.

10.   Fruit and Peanut Butter Smoothie

What better way to get your day's worth of calcium than with this strawberry flavored smoothie? High in minerals, vitamins, protein and energy fueling carbs, this smoothie is a perfect way to kick-start your day.

Ingredients (1 serving):

15 medium-sized strawberries

1 1/3 tablespoons peanut butter

85g tofu

½ cup fat free yogurt

¾ cup skim milk

1 scoop protein powder

8 ice cubes

Prep time: 5min

No cooking

Preparation:

Pour the milk into the blender then the yogurt and the rest of the ingredients. Blend until mixture is completely blended and frothy. Pour into a glass and serve.

Nutritional value per serving: 472kcal, 45g protein, 40g carbs (6g fiber, 31g sugar), 13g fat (4g saturated), 110% calcium, 35% iron, 27% magnesium, 30% vitamin A, 190% vitamin C, 11% vitamin E, 13% vitamin B1, 24% vitamin B2, 10% vitamin B5, 18% vitamin B6, 17% vitamin B9, 12% vitamin B12.

11.   Whey Protein Muffins

With a healthy dose of oats and a serving of chocolate whey protein powder, these muffins are a great breakfast alternative to regular oats. Paired with a glass of milk, this meal makes sure that you get a good amount of calcium and vitamin D to go with the nice protein and carbs serving.

Ingredients (4 muffins-2 servings):

1 cup rolled oats

1 large whole egg

5 large egg whites

½ scoop chocolate whey protein powder

olive oil spray

2 cups of low fat milk, to serve

Prep time: 2 min

Cooking time: 15 min

Preparation:

Preheat the oven to 190C fan/ gas 5.

Blend all the ingredients together for 30s. Spray the muffin tin with olive oil then batter up into four muffins. Place in the oven for 15 min.

Remove from the oven, let them cool and serve with the glass of milk.

Nutritional value per serving (includes milk): 330kcal, 28g protein, 37g carbs (9g fiber, 13g sugar), 6g fat (5g saturated), 37% calcium, 22% iron, 19% magnesium, 12% vitamin A, 34% vitamin D, 44% vitamin B1, 66% vitamin B2, 25% vitamin B5, 11% vitamin B6, 24% vitamin B12.

12.   Smoked Salmon and Avocado with Toast

Are you in for a tough workout and low on time? It only takes 5 min to piece together this savory breakfast. Both the salmon and avocado are high in healthy acids and this meal has enough protein and carbs to keep you motivated.

Ingredients (2 servings):

300g smoked salmon

2 medium-sized ripe avocados, stoned and peeled

Juice from ½ lemon

handful tarragon leaves, chopped

2 slices of whole wheat bread, toasted

Prep time: 5 min

No cooking time

Preparation:

Cut the avocados into chunks and toss in the lemon juice. Twist and fold the smoked salmon pieces, place them on serving plates, then scatter with the avocado and tarragon. Serve with whole wheat toast.

Nutritional value per serving: 550kcal, 34g protein, 37g carbs (12g fiber, 4g sugar), 30g fat (5g saturated), 17% iron, 24% magnesium, 25% vitamin C, 27% vitamin E, 42% vitamin K, 16% vitamin B1, 24% vitamin B2, 55% vitamin B3, 35% vitamin B5, 40% vitamin B6, 35% vitamin B9, 81% vitamin B12.

13. Breakfast 'Pizza'

Forget about the high-calorie, non-nutritious slice of pizza and replace it with this delicious substitute. Healthy and filling, it only takes 20 min to make and it's not only high in protein, but also in minerals and vitamins.

Ingredients (1 serving):

1 small whole wheat pita

3 egg whites

1 egg

¼ cup low-fat mozzarella cheese

1 spring onion, sliced

¼ cup mushrooms, diced

¼ cup bell peppers, diced

2 slices turkey bacon, chopped

1 teaspoon olive oil

salt and pepper

Prep time: 10 min

Cooking time: 10 min

Preparation:

Whisk the eggs with a pinch of salt and pepper and add the diced vegetables.

Bend the edges of the pita bread to create a bowl. Brush both sides with the olive oil and place the pita bread on the grill, dome side down. Cook until golden then flip it on the other side.

Pour the egg mix into the pita and cook until the eggs are nearly done, add the turkey bacon, spring onion and cheese. Cook until the cheese had melted and serve.

Nutritional value per serving: 350kcal, 33g protein, 12g carbs (3g fiber, 4g sugar), 15g fat (6 saturated), 32% calcium, 19% iron, 15% magnesium, 36% vitamin A, 88% vitamin C, 72% vitamin K, 21% vitamin B1, 71% vitamin B2, 22% vitamin B3, 14% vitamin B5, 21% vitamin B6, 25% vitamin B9, 29% vitamin B12.

14.   Mexican Mocha Breakfast

Top your favorite cup of oats with a healthy serving of almond milk and enjoy a quickly-made high-fiber breakfast. The cayenne pepper is perfect for adding a little oomph to your oatmeal.

Ingredients (1 serving):

½ cup rolled oats

1 scoop chocolate protein powder

½ tablespoon cinnamon

½ teaspoon cayenne pepper

1 cup unsweetened almond milk

1 tablespoon unsweetened cocoa powder

Prep time: 5 min

Cooking time: 3 min

Preparation:

Mix all the ingredients in a microwave-safe bowl. Heat in the microwave for 2 ½ -3 min then serve.

Nutritional value per serving: 304kcal, 27g protein, 38g carbs (8g fiber, 3g sugar), 7g fat, 32% calcium, 15% iron, 25% magnesium, 10% vitamin A, 25% vitamin D, 51% vitamin E, 12% vitamin B1.

15.   Blueberry Lemon Pancakes

A warm, filling breakfast, this blueberry pancake enriched by the lemony flavor is a simple and tasty way of getting that high-powered meal that you need to start your day. Spread a tablespoon of Greek yogurt on top of your pancake if you like.

Ingredients (1 serving):

1/3 cup oat bran

5 egg whites

½ cup blueberries

1 scoop flavorless whey protein powder

½ teaspoon baking soda

1 teaspoon grated lemon peel

1 tablespoon lemon drink mix

olive oil spray

Prep time: 5 min

Cooking time: 5 min

Preparation:

Combine all the ingredients in a large bowl, mix and whisk until smooth.

Cook the batch in a sprayed skilled on medium-high temperature until bubbles form on the surface. Flip over and cook until each side is dark golden brown. Remove the pancake and serve.

Nutritional value per serving: 340kcal, 47g protein, 37g carbs (6g fiber, 14g sugar), 5g fat, 10% iron, 25% magnesium, 12% vitamin C, 19% vitamin K, 26% vitamin B1, 58% vitamin B2.

LUNCH

16.   Mediterranean Rice

Turn the tired can of tuna into a delicious dish that is a perfect starter for an afternoon of exercise. The high amount of carbs will fuel a thorough workout and the protein will make sure that your muscles recuperate from the effort.

Ingredients (1 serving):

1 can of tuna in oil, drained

100g brown rice

¼ avocado, chopped

¼ red onion, sliced

juice from ½ lemon

salt and pepper

Prep time: 5 min

Cooking time: 20 min

Preparation:

Boil the brown rice for approximately 20 min then place in a bowl with the onion, tuna and avocado. Add the lemon juice and mix all the ingredients. Season with salt and pepper to taste and serve.

Nutritional value per serving: 590kcal, 32g protein, 80g carbs (7g fiber, 1g sugar), 14g fat (5g saturated), 22% iron, 52% magnesium, 101% vitamin D, 18% vitamin E, 107% vitamin K, 32% vitamin B1, 134% vitamin B3, 26% vitamin B5, 39% vitamin B6, 15% vitamin B9, 63% vitamin B12.

17.   Spiced Chicken

Chicken is perfect for a high protein muscle building meal. High in nutrients across the board, this simple, tasty meal can be paired with a serving of your choice of carbs.

Ingredients (2 servings):

3 boneless chicken breasts cut in half

175g low-fat yogurt

5cm piece cucumber, finely chopped

2 tablespoons Thai red curry paste

2 tablespoons cilantro, chopped

2 cups raw spinach, to serve.

Prep time: 5 min

Cooking time: 35-40 min

Preparation:

Preheat the oven to 190C fan/ gas 5. Put the chicken in a dish in one layer. Blend a third of the yogurt, the curry paste and two thirds of the cilantro, add salt and pour over the chicken, making sure the meat is evenly coated. Leave for 30 min (or in the fridge overnight).

Lift the chicken onto a rack in a roasting tin for 35-40 min, until golden.

Heat water in a pan and wilt the spinach.

Mix the rest of the yogurt and cilantro, add the cucumber and stir. Pour the mix over the chicken and serve with the cooked spinach.

Nutritional value per serving: 275kcal, 43g protein, 8g carbs (1g fiber, 8g sugar), 3g fat (1g saturated), 20% calcium, 15% iron, 25% magnesium, 56% vitamin A, 18% vitamin C, 181% vitamin K, 16% vitamin B1, 26% vitamin B2, 133% vitamin B3, 25% vitamin B5, 67% vitamin B6, 19% vitamin B9, 22% vitamin B12.

18.   Stuffed Eggs with Pita Bread

Get your fill of omega-3 fatty acids with this rich salmon dish. High in vitamins and minerals, this filling meal is a great way of boosting yourself with energy and powering through your day.

Ingredients (2 servings):

1 canned salmon in water (450g)

2 eggs

1 large spring onions, finely chopped

2 large leafs of lettuce

10 cherry tomatoes

1 tablespoon Greek yogurt

a large whole wheat pita bread, cut in half

sea salt and pepper

Prep time: 10 min

Cooking time: 10 min

Preparation:

Boil the eggs, peel them and slice them in half then remove the yolks and place them in a bowl.

Add the canned salmon, 1 tablespoon of yogurt, the spring onion and the seasonings to the bowl. Mix all the ingredients together and stuff the egg whites. Serve with pita bread stuffed with lettuce and tomatoes.

Nutritional value per serving: 455kcal, 45g protein, 24g carbs (3g fiber, 2g sugar), 36g fat (10g saturated), 59% calcium, 22% iron, 21% magnesium, 30% vitamin A, 24% vitamin C, 43% vitamin K, 11% vitamin B1, 36% vitamin B2, 60% vitamin B3, 20% vitamin B5, 41% vitamin B6, 20% vitamin B9, 20% vitamin B12.

19.   Chicken Caesar Wraps

These chicken wraps make a great portable meal that will make sure that you keep your protein levels high throughout the day. Throw in some baby spinach and make a more green friendly meal.

Ingredients (1 serving):

85g chicken breast, baked

2 whole wheat tortillas

1 cup lettuce

50g non-fat yogurt

1 teaspoon anchovy paste

1 teaspoon dry mustard powder

1 clove garlic, cooked

½ medium cucumber, chopped

Prep time: 5 min

No cooking

Preparation:

Combine the anchovy paste, garlic and yogurt then toss and coat the lettuce and cucumbers. Split the mix in 2, add to the tortillas and then place half the chicken in each tortilla. Wrap up and serve.

Nutritional value per serving (2 tortillas): 460kcal, 41g protein, 57g carbs (7g fiber, 9g sugar), 10g fat (2g saturated), 11% calcium, 22% vitamin K, 13% vitamin B2, 59% vitamin B3, 12% vitamin B5, 29% vitamin B6, 10% vitamin B12.

20.   Baked Salmon with Grilled Asparagus

A classic dish, made more interesting by a marinade of lemon juice and mustard, this grilled salmon goes well with the garlicky asparagus spears. Treat yourself to a great combination of protein and vitamins.

Ingredients (1 serving):

140g wild salmon

1 ½ cup asparagus

Marinade:

1 tablespoon garlic, minced

1 tablespoon Dijon mustard

lemon juice from ½ lemon

1 teaspoon olive oil

Prep time: 5 min

Cooking time: 15 min

Preparation:

Preheat oven to 200C fan/ gas 6.

In a bowl, mix the lemon juice, half the garlic, olive oil and mustard, pour the marinade over the salmon and make sure it is completely covered. Place the marinating salmon in the fridge for at least one hour.

Cut the bottom stems off the asparagus spears. Set a nonstick skillet on medium/high heat, toss the asparagus with the remaining garlic and sear for about 5 min, rolling the asparagus on all sides.

Place the salmon on a baking sheet and bake for 10 min then serve with the grilled asparagus.

Nutritional value: 350kcal, 43g protein, 7g carbs (5g fiber, 1 g sugar), 16g fat (1 saturated), 17% iron, 20% magnesium, 48% vitamin A, 119% vitamin C, 17% vitamin E, 288% vitamin K, 39% vitamin B1, 60% vitamin B2, 90% vitamin B3, 33% vitamin B5, 74% vitamin B6, 109% vitamin B9, 75% vitamin B12.

21.   Beef Meatball Pasta with Spinach

A high-protein pasta meal that makes the most of the beef and spinach pairing. Not only is it all-round vitamin packed, but it also contains a hearty amount of magnesium which helps regulate muscle contraction.

Ingredients (2 servings):

For meatballs:

170g lean ground beef

½ cup raw spinach, shredded

1 tablespoon minced garlic

¼ cup red onion, diced

1 teaspoon cumin

sea salt and pepper

For Pasta:

100g wheat spinach pasta

10 cherry tomatoes

2 cups raw spinach

¼ cup marinara

2 tablespoons low-fat parmesan cheese

Prep time: 15 min

Cooking time: 30 min

Preparation:

Preheat oven to 200C/ gas 6.

Mix together the ground beef, raw spinach, garlic, red onion and salt and pepper to taste. Mix thoroughly with your hands until the spinach is completely mixed into the meat.

Form two or three meatballs, roughly the same size then place them on a baking sheet in the oven for 10-12 minutes.

Cook the pasta according to the instructions on the pack. Drain the pasta and stir in the tomatoes, spinach and cheese. Add the meatballs and serve.

Nutritional value per serving: 470kcal, 33g protein, 50g carbs (6g fiber, 5g sugar), 12g fat (5g saturated), 17% calcium, 28% iron, 74% magnesium, 104% vitamin A, 38% vitamin C, 11% vitamin E, 361% vitamin K, 16% vitamin B1,

20% vitamin B2, 45% vitamin B3, 11% vitamin B5, 45% vitamin B6, 35% vitamin B9, 37% vitamin B12.

22.   Stuffed Chicken Breast with Brown Rice

Brown rice is an excellent way of introducing quality carbs to your diet. Couple it with high-protein chicken breast and some vegetables and you have a delicious power lunch.

Ingredients (1 serving):

170g chicken breast

½ cup raw spinach

50g brown rice

1 spring onion, diced

1 tomato, sliced

1 tablespoon feta cheese

Prep time: 10 min

Cooking time: 30 min

Preparation:

Preheat the oven to 190C fan/ gas 5.

Slice the chicken breast down the middle to make it look like a butterfly. Season the chicken with salt and pepper, then open it and layer spinach, feta cheese and tomato slices on one side. Fold the chicken breast and use a toothpick to hold it closed then bake for 20 min.

Boil the brown rice then add the garlic and chopped onion. Fill a plate with brown rice, place the chicken on top and serve.

Nutritional value per serving: 469kcal, 48g protein, 46g carbs (5g fiber, 6g sugar), 8g fat (5g saturated), 22% calcium, 18% iron, 38% magnesium, 55% vitamin A, 43% vitamin C, 169% vitamin K, 28% vitamin B1, 28% vitamin B2, 103% vitamin B3, 28% vitamin B5, 70% vitamin B6, 23% vitamin B9, 17% vitamin B12.

23.   Shrimp and Zucchini Linguine Pasta Salad

A cheat pasta meal with a serving of shredded zucchini and steamed shrimp flavored with all manners of sesame. This combination of ingredients makes for a light lunch with a high-protein content.

Ingredients (1 serving):

170g steamed shrimp

1 large zucchini, chopped

¼ cup red onion, sliced

1 cup bell peppers, sliced

1 tablespoon roasted Tahini butter

1 teaspoon sesame oil

1 teaspoon sesame seeds

Prep time: 10 min

No cooking

Preparation:

Cut the zucchini using a shredder in order to make raw linguine.

In a bowl, mix tahini and sesame oil.

Place all the ingredients in a large bowl, pour the Tahini sauce and toss it to make sure all sides are covered in sauce. Sprinkle some sesame seeds and serve.

Nutritional value per serving: 420kcal, 45g protein, 26g carbs (10g fiber, 12g sugar), 18g fat (2g saturated), 19% calcium, 47% iron, 48% magnesium, 33% vitamin A, 303% vitamin C, 17% vitamin E, 31% vitamin K, 38% vitamin B1, 36% vitamin B2, 38% vitamin B3, 13% vitamin B5, 66% vitamin B6, 35% vitamin B9, 42% vitamin B12.

24. Turkey Meatloaf with Whole Wheat Couscous

Cooked in a muffin pan, this turkey meatloaf makes sure that you minimize you saturated fats intake. Mix it up a little by adding bell pepper or mushrooms instead of onion into the meatballs and by seasoning with a pinch of ground garlic.

Ingredients (1 serving):

140g lean ground turkey

¾ cup red onions, diced

1 cup raw spinach

1/3 cup low sodium marinara sauce

½ cup whole wheat couscous, boiled

choice of seasoning: Parsley, Basil, Coriander

pepper, salt

olive oil spray

Prep time: 5 min

Cooking time: 20 min

Preparation:

Preheat oven to 200C fan/ gas 6.

Season turkey with your choice of seasoning and add the diced onions.

Light spray your muffin pan with olive oil, place the ground turkey inside the muffin holders. Top each turkey meatball with 1 tablespoon marinara sauce, then place in the oven and bake for 8-10 min.

Serve with couscous.

Nutritional value per serving: 460kcal, 34g protein, 53g carbs (4g fiber, 7g sugar), 12g fat (4g saturated), 12% calcium, 15% iron, 10% magnesium, 16% vitamin A, 15% vitamin C, 11% vitamin E, 16% vitamin K, 11% vitamin B1, 25% vitamin B3, 16% vitamin B6, 11% vitamin B9.

25.   Tuna Burger and Salad

The tuna burger is high in protein and carbs, making it an excellent choice for a workout day meal. Fix it differently every time and keep it interesting by switching between vegetables and seasoning your salad dressing.

Ingredients (1 serving):

1 canned chunk tuna (165g)

1 egg white

½ cup chopped mushrooms

2 cups lettuce, shredded

¼ cup dried oats

1 teaspoon olive oil

1 tablespoons low-fat salad dressing (of preference)

small bunch of oregano, chopped

1 whole wheat medium roll cut in half

Prep time: 10 min

Cooking time: 10 min

Preparation:

Mix together the egg white, tuna, dry oats, oregano and form a patty.

Heat the oil in a non-stick pan on medium heat, place the patty on and flip it to make sure it cooks on both sides.

Cut the whole wheat roll in half, horizontally, place the patty between the 2 pieces.

Mix the vegetables in a bowl, add the salad dressing and serve next to the tuna burger.

Nutritional value per serving: 560kcal, 52g protein, 76g carbs (13g fiber, 7g sugar), 10g fat (1g saturated), 11% calcium, 35% iron, 38% magnesium, 16% vitamin A, 16% vitamin K, 35% vitamin B1, 33% vitamin B2, 24% vitamin B3, 28% vitamin B5, 41% vitamin B6, 21% vitamin B9, 82% vitamin B12.

26.   Spicy Beefsteak Kebabs

This spicy kebab is served with a side of baked potato, making it not only a muscle building meal but also a great way of introducing eyesight protecting vitamin A to your diet. Add a tablespoon of low-fat yogurt to your potato to make it more refreshing.

Ingredients (1 serving):

140g lean beef flank steak

200g sweet potato

1 bell pepper, chopped

½ medium zucchini, chopped

minced garlic

pepper, salt

Prep time: 15 min

Cooking time: 55 min

Preparation:

Preheat oven to 200C fan/ gas 6. Wrap the sweet potato in a foil, place in the oven and bake for 45 min.

Cut the flank steak into small pieces, season with salt, pepper and garlic. Assemble the kebab, alternating between beef, zucchini and bell pepper.

Place the kebab on a baking sheet and bake for 10 min. Serve with the sweet potato.

Nutritional value per serving: 375kcal, 38g protein, 49g carbs (9g fiber, 12g sugar), 4g fat (1g saturated), 24% iron, 27% magnesium, 581% vitamin A, 195% vitamin C, 21% vitamin K, 22% vitamin B1, 28% vitamin B2, 61% vitamin B3, 28% vitamin B5, 92% vitamin B6, 20% vitamin B9, 30% vitamin B12.

27.   Trout with Potatoes Salad

Want to make sure that you are not lacking in vitamin B12? Try this hearty portion of trout, paired with a nutrient and vitamin packed fresh-tasting potato salad.

Ingredients (2 servings):

2*140g trout fillets

250g waxy potatoes, halved

4 teaspoons yogurt

4 teaspoons reduced-fat mayonnaise

1 tablespoon capers, rinsed

4 small cornichons, sliced

2 spring onions, finely sliced

¼ cucumber, diced

1 lemon, zest from ½

Prep time: 10 min

Cooking time: 20 min

Preparation:

Boil the potatoes in salted water for 15 min until they are just tender. Drain and rinse under cold water, then drain again.

Heat the grill.

Mix the mayonnaise and yogurt and season with some lemon juice. Stir the mix into the potatoes with the capers, most of the spring onion, cucumber and cornichons. Scatter the salad with the rest of the onions.

Season the trout, grill on a baking sheet, skin-side down, until just cooked. Scatter with the lemon zest and serve with the potato salad.

Nutritional value per serving: 420kcal, 38g protein, 28g carbs (3g fiber, 6g sugar), 13g fat (3g saturated), 12% calcium, 11% iron, 22% magnesium, 29% vitamin C, 59% vitamin K, 21% vitamin B1, 18% vitamin B2, 12% vitamin B3, 22% vitamin B5, 43% vitamin B6, 18% vitamin B9, 153% vitamin B12.

28.   Mexican Bean Chili

A high in protein midday meal, this dish is a great way of getting 1/3 of your daily required amount of fiber. Though it has enough nutrients to be a stand-alone meal, it can also be served on top of a bed of brown rice.

Ingredients (2 servings):

250g minced beef

200g caned baked beans

75ml beef stock

½ onion, diced

½ red pepper, diced

1 teaspoon chipotle paste

1 teaspoon olive oil

½ teaspoon chili powder

1 cup brown rice, boiled (optional)

coriander leaves, o serve

Prep time: 5 min

Cooking time: 45 min

Preparation:

Heat the oil in a non-stick pan over medium heat then fry the onion and red pepper until softened. Increase the heat, add the chili powder and cook for 2 min before adding the minced beef. Cook until browned and all the liquid has evaporated.

Tip in the beef stock, baked beans and chipotle paste. Simmer over a low heat for 20 min, then season and scatter with coriander leaves and serve with the boiled rice.

Nutritional value per serving (without rice): 402kcal, 34g protein, 19g carbs (5g fiber, 10g sugar), 14g fat (5g saturated), 29% iron, 15% magnesium, 42% vitamin C, 11% vitamin B1, 16% vitamin B2, 34% vitamin B3, 40% vitamin B6, 18% vitamin B9, 52% vitamin B12.

½ cup of rice: 108kcal

29.   Beef and Broccoli Noodles

A convenient, tasty dish, the beef and broccoli noodles take only 20 min to prepare, making it a great choice for a busy day. You can serve with a few slices of red chili for some extra spice.

Ingredients (2 servings):

2 cups egg noodles

200g beef stir-fry strips

1 spring onion, sliced

½ head broccoli, small florets

1 teaspoon sesame oil

For the sauce:

1 ½ tablespoons low-salt soy sauce

1 teaspoon tomato ketchup

1 garlic clove, crushed

1 tablespoon oyster sauce

¼ knob ginger, finely grated

1 teaspoon white wine vinegar

Prep time: 10 min

Cooking time: 10 min

Preparation:

Mix the ingredients for the sauce. Boil the noodles according to the pack instructions. Tip in the broccoli when they are almost ready. Leave for a few minutes then drain the noodles and broccoli.

Heat the oil in a wok until very hot then stir-fry the beef for 2-3 minutes until browned. Tip the sauce, stir, and let it simmer for a few moments then turn off the heat.

Stir the beef into the noodles, scatter with the spring onion and serve immediately.

Nutritional value per serving: 352kcal, 33g protein, 39g carbs (5g fiber, 5g sugar), 9g fat (2g saturated), 20% iron, 20% magnesium, 20% vitamin A, 224% vitamin C, 214% vitamin K, 14% vitamin B1, 19% vitamin B2, 43% vitamin B3, 18% vitamin B5, 50% vitamin B6, 31% vitamin B9, 23% vitamin B12.

30.   Pancetta-wrapped Pollock with Potatoes

This light and fresh-tasting dish provides a lot of energy and is high in protein, making it an ideal option for a midday meal. The pollock can be substituted for another sustainable white fish, while the olives can be replaced by sundried tomatoes.

Ingredients (2 servings):

2* 140g pollock fillets

4 slices pancetta

300g new potatoes

100g green beans

30g kalamata olives

juice and zest from 1 lemon

2 tablespoons olive oil

a few tarragon sprigs, leaves picked

Prep time: 10 min

Cooking time 15 min

Preparation:

Heat oven to 200C fan/ gas 6. Boil the potatoes for 10-12 min until tender, add the beans for the final 2-3 min. Drain well, slice the potatoes in half and tip into a baking dish. Toss with the olives, lemon zest and oil and season well.

Season the fish and wrap with the pancetta then place it on top of the potatoes. Bake for 10-12 min until cooked through, then add the lemon juice, scatter with tarragon and serve.

Nutritional value per serving: 525kcal, 46g protein, 36g carbs (5g fiber, 3g sugar), 31g fat (8g saturated), 10% iron, 31% magnesium, 63% vitamin C, 18% vitamin K, 15% vitamin B1, 13% vitamin B2, 14% vitamin B3, 25% vitamin B6, 73% vitamin B12.

DINNER

31.   Sushi Bowl

A low-calorie sushi bowl that substitutes rice for cauliflower flavored with garlic, soy sauce and lime juice for extra taste. Use the seaweed sheets to wrap the veggies and salmon and make a mini roll.

Ingredients (2 servings):

170g smoked salmon

1 medium-sized avocado

½ head cauliflower, steamed and chopped

1/3 cup carrot, shredded

½ teaspoon cayenne

1.2 teaspoon garlic powder

1 tablespoon low-sodium soy sauce

2 seaweed sheets

Juice from ½ lime

Prep time: 10 min

No cooking

Preparation:

Place the cauliflower, carrots, soy sauce, garlic, lime juice and cayenne in a food processor. Stop blending before the mix turns into a paste. Serve next to the salmon and seaweed sheets.

Nutritional value per serving: 272kcal, 20g protein, 13g carbs (7g fiber, 4g sugar), 16g fat (1g saturated), 10% iron, 14% magnesium, 73% vitamin A, 88% vitamin C, 13% vitamin E, 40% vitamin K, 18% vitamin B1, 15% vitamin B2, 31% vitamin B3, 21% vitamin B5, 31% vitamin B6, 26% vitamin B9, 45% vitamin B12.

32.   Sweet and Sour Chicken

The sweet and sour chicken is a simple, delicious recipe that has a place in every fit kitchen. It is high in protein and vitamins and goes well with steamed broccoli florets.

Ingredients (2 servings):

300g chicken breasts cut into bite-sized pieces

1 teaspoon garlic salt

¼ cup low sodium chicken broth

¼ cup white vinegar

¼ no-calorie sweetener

¼ teaspoon black pepper

1 teaspoon low-sodium soy sauce

3 teaspoons low-sugar ketchup

arrowroot

400g broccoli florets, steamed

Prep time: 10 min

Cooking time 15 min

Preparation:

Place the chicken in a large bowl and season with the garlic, pepper and salt, turning to coat. Cook the chicken over medium/high heat until done.

In the meantime, whisk together the chicken broth, sweetener, vinegar, ketchup and soy sauce in a sauce pan, bring the mix to a boil and turn to low heat. Add the arrowroot a little at a time and whisk briskly. Keep stirring for a few minutes.

Pour sauce over the cooked chicken and serve with a side of steamed broccoli.

Nutritional value per serving: 250kcal, 40g protein, 14g carbs (6g fiber, 4g sugar), 2g fat, 11% calcium, 14% iron, 20% magnesium, 24% vitamin A, 303% vitamin C, 254% vitamin K, 17% vitamin B1, 21% vitamin B2, 90% vitamin B3, 24% vitamin B5, 58% vitamin B6, 33% vitamin B9.

33.   Garlicky Hummus

You only need 5 min to make this healthy, delicious meal. It is chock-full with magnesium and has a decent amount of protein considering the recipe is meatless. Grab a whole wheat tortilla and make this meal to go.

Ingredients (3 servings):

1*400g canned chickpeas (save1/4 of the liquid)

¼ cup tahini

¼ cup lemon juice

1 clove garlic

1 tablespoon olive oil

¼ teaspoon ground ginger

¼ teaspoon ground cumin

2 spring onions, finely chopped

1 tomato, chopped

Prep time: 5 min

No cooking

Preparation:

Place the chickpeas, liquid, tahini, lemon juice, olive oil, garlic, cumin and ginger in a food processor and blend until smooth.

Stir in the tomato and scallions and season with salt and pepper. Serve next to slices of bell pepper.

Nutritional value per serving: 324kcal, 11g protein, 21g carbs (7g fiber, 1g sugar), 17g fat (2g saturated), 22% calcium, 54% iron, 135% magnesium, 10% vitamin A, 12% vitamin C, 33% vitamin K, 122% vitamin B1, 12% vitamin B2, 44% vitamin B3, 11% vitamin B5, 12% vitamin B6, 40% vitamin B9.

34.   Chicken with Pineapple and Bell Peppers

Take a break from the usual chicken recipes and try this version with sweet, fresh pineapple. High in vitamin B3 and protein, this meal is also an important source of carbs. In tone with the change of pace, you can substitute the rice for quinoa.

Ingredients (1 serving):

140g boneless chicken breast,

1 tablespoon mustard

½ cup fresh pineapple, diced

½ cup bell peppers, diced

50g brown rice

Coconut oil spray

1 teaspoon cumin

salt and pepper

Prep time: 5 min

Cooking time: 15 min

Preparation:

Cut the chicken into small pieces then rub the mustard on the pieces and season with salt, pepper and cumin.

Set a skillet on medium heat and lightly spray with coconut oil, add the chicken and cook on all sides. When the chicken is almost finished, increase the heat and toss in the pineapple pieces and bell peppers, cook and make sure that all sides are brown. This should take 3-5 min.

Boil the brown rice and serve next to the chicken.

Nutritional value per serving: 377kcal, 37g protein, 50g carbs (6g fiber, 10g sugar), 1g fat, 12% iron, 33% magnesium, 168% vitamin C, 26% vitamin B1, 13% vitamin B2, 96% vitamin B3, 22% vitamin B5, 65% vitamin B6, 10% vitamin B9.

35.   Mexican Style Protein Bowl

Give yourself a break from meat and throw these ingredients together for a tasty alternative to the usual. You can skip the fried fat and unhealthy calories and still get the flavor of a Mexican meal.

Ingredients:

1/3 cup cooked black beans

½ cup cooked brown rice

2 tablespoons salsa

¼ avocado, sliced

Prep time: 5 min

No cooking

Preparation:

Combine all the ingredients in a bowl and serve.

Nutritional value per serving: 307kcal, 11g protein, 48g carbs (11g fiber, 1g sugar), 7g fat (1g sugar), 26%

magnesium, 13% vitamin K, 16% vitamin B1, 11% vitamin B3, 17% vitamin B6, 30% vitamin B9.

36.   Arugula Chicken Salad

The arugula leaves add satisfaction to this sweet and super healthy salad. Bountiful in vegetables and quality protein source, this meal can be enriched with a simple dressing of low-fat yogurt and garlic.

Ingredients (1 serving):

120g chicken breast

5 baby carrots, chopped

¼ red cabbage, chopped

½ cup arugula

1 tablespoon sunflower seeds

1 teaspoon olive oil

Prep time: 10 min

Cooking time: 10 min

Preparation:

Cut the chicken into bite-sized cubes. Heat the olive oil in a non-stick pan and fry the chicken until it is cooked. Set aside and allow cooling.

Place the carrots, arugula and cabbage in a large bowl. Top the salad with the cooled chicken and sunflower seeds and serve.

Nutritional value per serving: 311kcal, 30g protein, 9g carbs (1g fiber), 13g fat (1g saturated), 11% iron, 22% magnesium, 150% vitamin A, 25% vitamin C, 29% vitamin E, 32% vitamin K, 23% vitamin B1, 10% vitamin B2, 72% vitamin B3, 11% vitamin B5, 49% vitamin B6, 17% vitamin B9.

37.   Dijon Mustard Halibut

This tangy halibut meal is a fast-and-easy way to get a hearty dose of protein. It's low in carbs and high in vitamins, making it a perfect choice for supper. The low calorie count allows you to double the sauce if you are feeling indulgent.

Ingredients (2 servings):

220g halibut

¼ onion, diced

1 red pepper, diced

1 clove garlic

1 tablespoon Dijon mustard

1 teaspoon Worcestershire sauce

1 teaspoon olive oil

juice from 1 lemon

a bunch of parsley

2 large carrots cut into sticks

1 cup broccoli florets

1 cup mushrooms, sliced

Prep time: 10 min

Cooking time: 20 min

Preparation:

Place the red pepper, garlic, parsley, mustard, onion Worcestershire sauce, lemon juice and olive oil in a food processor.

Place the fish, sauce and the rest of the vegetables in a large parchment baking bag. Bake at 190C fan/ gas 5 for 20 min then serve.

Nutritional value per serving: 225kcal, 33g protein, 12g carbs (3g fiber, 5g sugar), 5g fat (1g saturated), 11% calcium, 10% iron, 35% magnesium, 180% vitamin A, 77% vitamin C, 71% vitamin K, 13% vitamin B1, 19% vitamin B2, 51% vitamin B3, 14% vitamin B5, 34% vitamin B6, 15% vitamin B9, 25% vitamin B12.

38.   Tray Bake Chicken

Quick, easy and tasty, this dish should be a summer staple in your kitchen since there is no shortage of fresh cherry tomatoes. The pesto adds a refreshing flavor to a simply seasoned chicken breast.

Ingredients (2 servings):

300g chicken breast

300g cherry tomatoes

2 tablespoons pesto

1 tablespoon olive oil

salt, pepper

Prep time: 5 min

Cooking time: 15 min

Preparation:

Place the chicken breast in a roasting tray, season, drizzle with the olive oil then grill for 10 min. Add the cherry tomatoes and grill for another 5 min until the chicken is cooked. Spread pesto over the top and serve next to the cherry tomatoes.

Nutritional value per serving: 312kcal, 36g protein, 7g carbs (2g fiber, 5g sugar), 19g fat (4g saturated), 15% magnesium, 25% vitamin A, 34% vitamin C, 11% vitamin E, 20% vitamin K, 10% vitamin B1, 88% vitamin B3, 13% vitamin B5, 33% vitamin B6.

39.   Tofu burger

Tofu has all of the essential amino acids, and that makes it a perfect substitute for meat. The caramelized onions with chili flakes and Sriracha, paired with the teriyaki infused tofu will delight your taste buds.

Ingredients (1 serving):

85g tofu (extra firm)

1 tablespoon teriyaki marinade

1 tablespoon Sriracha

1 lettuce leaf

30g carrot, shredded

¼ red onion, sliced

½ teaspoon red chili flakes

1 medium-sized whole wheat roll

Prep time: 5 min

Cooking time: 10 min

Preparation:

Heat the grill.

Marinate the tofu in teriyaki marinade, red chili flakes and Sriracha then grill it for 3-5 min on each side.

Fry the red onion in a non-stick pan until caramelized.

Cut the roll in half until you can open it like a book. Stuff the roll with the grilled tofu, caramelized onion, carrots and lettuce and serve.

Nutritional value per serving: 194kcal, 11g protein, 28g carbs (5g fiber, 8g sugar), 5g fat (1g saturated), 21% calcium, 14% iron, 19% magnesium, 95% vitamin A, 10% vitamin B1, 14% vitamin B6.

40.   Hot Cod

High in protein and healthy fats and low in carbs, this super spicy cod will give a jolt for the rest of your day. Serve it with a bit of brown rice if you need a carb boost for an evening workout and add 2 more peppers if you feel you can handle more spice.

Ingredients (2 servings):

340g white cod

10 cherry tomatoes, halved

2 jalapeno peppers, sliced

2 tablespoons olive oil

sea salt

chili powder

Prep time: 5 min

Cooking time: 10 min

Preparation:

Heat the oil in a non-stick pan. Coat the cod in salt and chili powder, add to the pan and cook for 10 min on medium heat. Toss in the peppers 1-2 min before the fish is cooked through.

Serve with cherry tomatoes.

Nutritional value per serving: 279kcal, 30g protein, 6g carbs (1g fiber, 1 g sugar), 16g fat (2g saturated), 11% magnesium, 17% vitamin A, 38% vitamin C, 26% vitamin E, 33% vitamin K, 24% vitamin B3, 43% vitamin B6, 26% vitamin B12.

41.   Grilled Mushroom and Zucchini Burger

The Portobello mushrooms have a thick, meaty texture that makes them a favorite among vegetarians and meat lovers alike. Indulge in nature's burger and get a load of minerals and vitamins at a minimal calorie cost.

Ingredients (1 serving):

1 large portabella mushroom cap

¼ small zucchini, sliced

1 teaspoon roasted bell peppers

1 slice of low fat cheese

4 spinach leaves

olive oil spray

1 medium-sized whole wheat roll

Prep time: 5 min

Cooking time: 5 min

Preparation:

Heat the grill. Spray the mushroom cap with olive oil then grill both mushroom and zucchini slices.

Cut the roll in half, horizontally, then place the ingredients in layers on one half and cover with the other. Serve immediately.

Nutritional value per serving: 185kcal, 12g protein, 24g carbs (4g fiber, 5g sugar), 4g fat (1g saturated), 21% calcium, 17% iron, 20% magnesium, 78% vitamin A, 28% vitamin C, 242% vitamin K, 15% vitamin B1, 37% vitamin B2, 26% vitamin B3, 16% vitamin B5, 16% vitamin B6, 31% vitamin B9.

42. Mediterranean Fish

What better way to reach your daily B12 requirement than with a dish bursting of Mediterranean flavors? The rest of the vitamins and minerals are also well represented and the protein count is at a good amount for a light supper.

Ingredients (2 servings):

200g fresh trout

2 medium-sized tomatoes

3 teaspoons capers

½ red bell pepper, chopped

1 garlic clove, chopped

10 green olives, sliced

¼ onion, chopped

½ cup spinach

1 tablespoon olive oil

salt and pepper

Prep time: 10 min

Cooking time: 15 min

Preparation:

Heat a large pan over medium heat; add whole tomatoes, garlic and olive oil. Cover and let it simmer for a few minutes until the tomatoes begin to soften.

Add the onion, bell pepper, olives, capers, salt and pepper (and a little water if necessary). Cover and let it simmer until the tomatoes have broken down and the bell pepper and onion have softened.

Add the trout, cover and poach for 5-7 min.

Add the spinach at the last minute then serve.

Nutritional value per serving: 305kcal, 24g protein, 7g carbs (1g fiber, 4g sugar), 11g fat (3g saturated), 10% calcium, 12% magnesium, 36% vitamin A, 56% vitamin C, 62% vitamin K, 13% vitamin B1, 33% vitamin B3, 12% vitamin B5, 25% vitamin B6, 15% vitamin B9, 105% vitamin B12.

43. Vegan friendly dinner

A vegan friendly meal with a good amount of protein and vitamins. Give your palate the taste it deserves with this sweet and spicy sauce that flavors a filling amount of tofu and is easy to make.

Ingredients (2 servings):

340g tofu

¼ cup soy sauce

¼ cup brown sugar

2 teaspoons sesame oil

1 teaspoon olive oil

1 teaspoon chili flakes

2 garlic cloves, minced

1 teaspoon ginger, freshly grated

salt

Prep time: 5 min

Cooking time: 15 min

Preparation:

Mix the brown sugar, soy sauce, sesame oil, ginger, chili flakes and salt in a bowl and set aside.

Pour olive oil into a sauce pan and heat then fry the tofu for about 10 min.

Pour the sauce into the pan and cook for 3-5 min. Serve when the sauce has thickened and the tofu is done.

Nutritional value per serving: 245kcal, 17g protein, 15g carbs (1g fiber, 11g sugar), 15g fat (3g saturated), 34% calcium, 19% iron, 19% magnesium, 11% vitamin B2, 11% vitamin B6.

44.   Tuna Melt

Unlike a regular tuna melt that is high in saturated fats and carbs, this one has a moderate amount of carbs and packs the protein-punch of a tuna can, making it an excellent meal that supports lean muscle growth.

Ingredients (2 servings):

1 can of tuna (165g)

2 slices of low-fat mozzarella cheese

2 teaspoons tomato sauce

1 whole wheat English muffin

a sprinkle of oregano

Prep time: 5 min

Cooking time: 3 min

Preparation:

Preheat the oven to 190C fan/ gas 5.

Slice the English muffin then smear each half with the tomato sauce. Top with the tuna, sprinkle with the oregano and place one slice of cheese on top of the tuna. Place the mini-melts in the oven and bake for 2-3 min or until the cheese has melted then divide between 2 plates and serve.

Nutritional value per serving: 255kcal, 31g protein, 14g carbs (2g fiber, 2 g sugar), 6g fat (4g saturated), 29% calcium, 11% iron, 13% magnesium, 10% vitamin B1, 10% vitamin B2, 60% vitamin B3, 23% vitamin B6, 52% vitamin B12.

45.   Chicken with Avocado Salad

A meal that provides a great balance of quality protein and healthy fats that will keep you satisfied without overdoing it on the carbs front. Replace the vinegar with lemon juice for a fresher feel.

Ingredients (1 serving):

100g chicken breast

1 teaspoon smoked paprika

2 teaspoons olive oil

For the salad:

½ medium avocado, diced

1 medium tomato, chopped

½ small red onion, thinly sliced

1 tablespoon parsley, roughly chopped

1 teaspoon red wine vinegar

Prep time: 10 min

Cooking time: 10 min

Preparation:

Heat the grill to medium. Rub the chicken with 1 teaspoon olive oil and paprika. Cook for 5 min on each side until it is cooked through and lightly charred. Cut the chicken in thick slices.

Mix the salad ingredients together, season, add the rest of the olive oil and serve with the chicken.

Nutritional value per serving: 346kcal, 26g protein, 14g carbs (6g fiber, 4g sugar), 22g fat (3g saturated), 16% magnesium, 22% vitamin, 44% vitamin C, 18% vitamin E, 38% vitamin K, 12% vitamin B1, 11% vitamin B2, 66% vitamin B3, 19% vitamin B5, 43% vitamin B6, 22% vitamin B9.

SNACKS

1. Cherry Tomatoes with Cottage Cheese

Cut 5 cherry tomatoes in half and smear them with 2 tablespoons goat cheese mixed with fresh dill and a pinch of salt.

Nutritional value: 58kcal, 4g protein, 10g carbs, 30% vitamin A, 40% vitamin C, 20% vitamin K, 10% vitamin B1, 10% vitamin B6, 10% vitamin B9.

2. Avocado on Toast

Toast a small piece of whole wheat bread then cover it with 50g of mashed avocado and sprinkle with salt and pepper.

Nutritional value: 208kcal, 5g protein, 28g carbs (6g fiber, 2g sugar), 9g fat (1g saturated), 13% vitamin K, 13% vitamin B9.

3. Bell Peppers with Cottage Cheese

Cut a small bell pepper in half, deseed it then stuff it with 50g cottage cheese mixed with your choice of seasoning.

Nutritional value: 44kcal, 6g protein, 3g carbs (3g sugar), 49% vitamin C.

4.   Rice Cake with Peanut Butter

Spread 1 rice cake with 1 tablespoon creamy peanut butter.

Nutritional value: 129kcal, 5g protein, 10g carbs (1g fiber, 1 g sugar), 8g fat (1g saturated), 10% vitamin B3.

5.   Celery Sticks with Goat Cheese and Green Olives

Top 3 medium celery sticks with 3 tablespoons goat cheese and 3 sliced green olives.

Nutritional value: 102kcal, 4g protein, 6g carbs (3g fiber), 6g fat (4g saturated), 12% calcium, 45% vitamin K, 18% vitamin A, 12% vitamin B9.

6.   Yogurt with Dried Goji Berries

Mix 150g low-fat yogurt with 10g goji berries.

Nutritional value: 134kcal, 7g protein, 19g carbs (1g fiber, 18% sugar), 4g fat (1g saturated), 27% calcium, 24% iron, 13% vitamin C, 19% vitamin B2, 13% vitamin B12.

7.   Apple and Peanut Butter

Slice 1 small apple and spread 1 tablespoon creamy peanut butter on the pieces.

Nutritional value: 189kcal, 4g protein, 28g carbs (5g fiber, 20g sugar), 8g fat (1g saturated), 14% vitamin C, 14% vitamin B3.

8. Greek Yogurt with Strawberries.

Mix 150g Greek Yogurt with 5 medium-sized strawberries cut in half.

Nutritional value: 150kcal, 11g protein, 10g carbs (10g sugar), 8g fat (5g saturated), 10% calcium, 60% vitamin C.

9. Nut Mix

Mix together 10g walnuts, 10g almond and 30g raisins.

Nutritional value: 217kcal, 4g protein, 25g carbs (2g fiber, 17g sugar), 13g fat (1g saturated), 10% magnesium.

10. Ham and Celery Sticks

Wrap 6 medium celery sticks with 3 slices of ham and serve with 1 teaspoon of whole grain mustard.

Nutritional value: 129kcal, 15g protein, 6g carbs (6g fiber), 3g fat, 12% calcium, 24% vitamin A, 12% vitamin C, 90% vitamin K, 18% vitamin B1, 12% vitamin B2, 24% vitamin B3, 15% vitamin B6, 24% vitamin B9.

11.　Yogurt with Tropical Fruit

Add 150g Greek Yogurt with ½ cup cut-up kiwi and ¼ cup cut-up mango.

Nutritional value: 210kcal, 12g protein, 25g carbs (2g fiber, 19g sugar), 8g fat (5g saturated), 13% calcium, 11% vitamin A, 155% vitamin C, 46% vitamin K.

12.　Blueberry Yogurt

Blend 150g low fat yogurt with ½ cup blueberries.

Nutritional value: 136kcal, 8g protein, 21g carbs (2g fiber, 18g sugar), 3g fat (1g saturated), 27% calcium, 13% vitamin C, 18% vitamin K, 21% vitamin B2, 13% vitamin B12.

13.　Cup of Popcorn

Nutritional value: 31kcal, 1g protein, 6g carbs (1g fiber).

14.　Roasted Chickpeas

Nutritional value 50g: 96kcal, 4g protein, 13g carbs (4g fiber, 2g sugar), 3g fat.

OTHER GREAT TITLES BY THIS AUTHOR

Advanced Mental Toughness Training for Bodybuilders

Using Visualization to Push Yourself to the Limit

By

Joseph Correa

Certified Sports Nutritionist

Becoming Mentally Tougher in Bodybuilding by Using Meditation

Reach Your Potential by Controlling Your Inner Thoughts

By

Joseph Correa

Certified Sports Nutritionist